# That FISH on your Dish

A book for children with eco-conscious parents

Researched and illustrated by: Ellen Marcus
Written and edited by: Ellen Marcus
and Dr. Sander Marcus

Copyright © 2011 Ellen Marcus & Sander Marcus
No part of this book may be reproduced in any form without written consent from the authors.

All rights reserved.

ACKNOWLEDGMENTS

Special thanks to Dr. Mark Sabaj Pérez, Dr. Jason Downs, and Nate Bender for their expert reviews.

Dedicated to my husband and family

All fishes depicted in this book should not be eaten because there are too few left in nature, or the methods used to catch them are destroying their habitat.

We hope these fish recover in such great numbers that they will no longer need to be represented in this book.

Foreword

By Ichthyologist Dr. Mark Sabaj Pérez
at The Academy of Natural Sciences,
Drexel University

    A beautiful book that will inspire young readers to stay curious and to become thoughtful stewards of the natural world. The choices they make are important, and this book informs such choices with engaging and playful illustrations and text. Only through such lessons can future generations hope to preserve what glorious life remains on Earth in its rivers, lakes and oceans, as well as on land and in the sky.

ORANGE ROUGHY

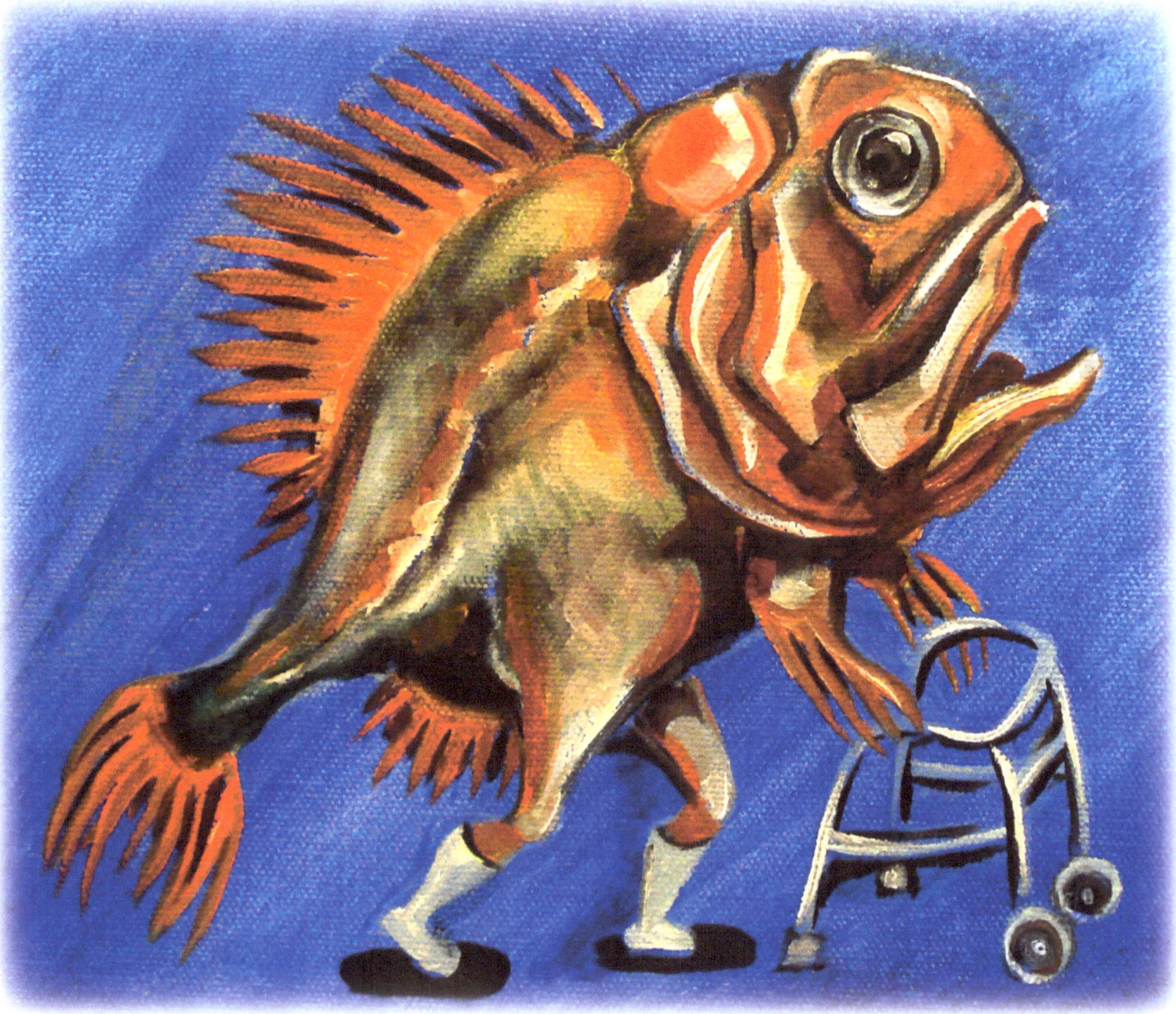

Scientific Name:
Hoplostethus atlanticus

It's obvious if you take a look,
This isn't the fastest fish in the ocean.
Whether it's swimming, or reading a book,
The Orange Roughy does everything slow motion.

STURGEON

Scientific Family:
Acipenseridae

The Sturgeon has no scales or teeth,
With skin that's hard like coal.
Searching the sand for what's beneath,
And swallowing its meals whole.

MENHADEN

Scientific Name:
Brevoortia tyrannus

The Menhaden is food for other fish,
And filters water pure.
In addition to being a favorite dish,
It's a great ecological cure.

SHARK

Scientific Superorder:
Selachimorpha

The electro-sensor of the shark
Really packs a punch.
It detects tiny movements in waters dark,
And can sense if you're its lunch.

PADDLEFISH

Scientific Family:
Polyodontidae

Named for that paddle-shaped nose.
With a mouth that opens wide.
And rarely if ever will close,
So its food has nowhere to hide.

STRIPED MARLIN

Scientific Name:
Tetrapturus audax

Chasing the Marlin can be a blast,
It will fight you with great power.
Oh sure, you can catch a fish that fast,
If your boat goes 60 miles an hour.

BLUEFIN TUNA

Scientific Genus:
Thunnus

Staying warm in degrees below one,
But why, we don't have an answer.
How can it weigh half a ton,
And glide like a ballet dancer?

EEL

Scientific Order:
Anguilliformes

Eels tend to work in a team,
Once they grow up and leave their mother,
They jump about as they swim upstream,
And, like ivy, they weave round each other.

SKATES and RAYS

Scientific Superorder:
Batoidea

The Skate and the Ray look alike, we've found,
And their shape, like a kite, is classic.
You can find their fossils in the ground,
Going back in time to the Jurassic.

CHILEAN SEABASS

Scientific Name:
Dissostichus eleginoides

Some fish live without need for heat,
The Chilean Sea Bass is one of these.
Its heart has a slow, sluggish beat,
And blood that acts like antifreeze.

**Scientific Name:
Lophius americanus**

The Monkfish has a light near its nose,
And as a beacon, it's a winner.
It draws small fish in close,
And then has them for dinner.

Add overfishing to pollution of the world's water,
And the red flags of danger are waving.
All fish are ripe for slaughter,
But all are special, and certainly worth saving.

The End

Do you wish to know more?
Then turn the page!

Fish Facts

In this section, you'll find additional facts to help you learn more about these amazing fish.

Orange Roughy

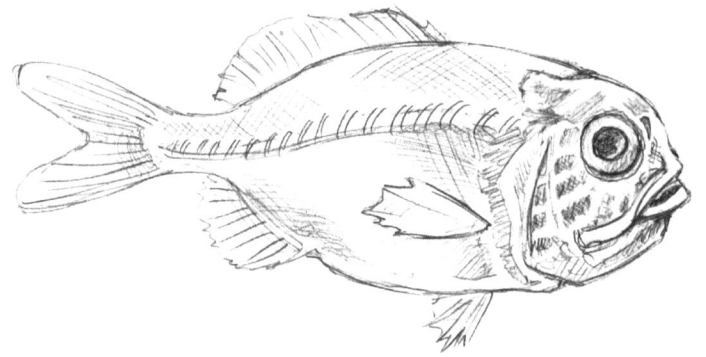

This fish was originally called the "Slimehead", but some people didn't think that a dish called "Slimehead" sounded very tasty, so they changed its name to Orange Roughy. It likes deep water where it is dark and cold. It can weigh about 15 pounds and live up to 150 years.

Sturgeon

These Fish don't have scales like other fish - they are covered with bony plates called "scutes". They rustle up the sand and dirt at the bottom of rivers and eat whatever swims out. Though they don't have teeth, and don't need them because they can swallow large salmon whole. They have survived the Arctic rivers unchanged for millions of years.

Sharks

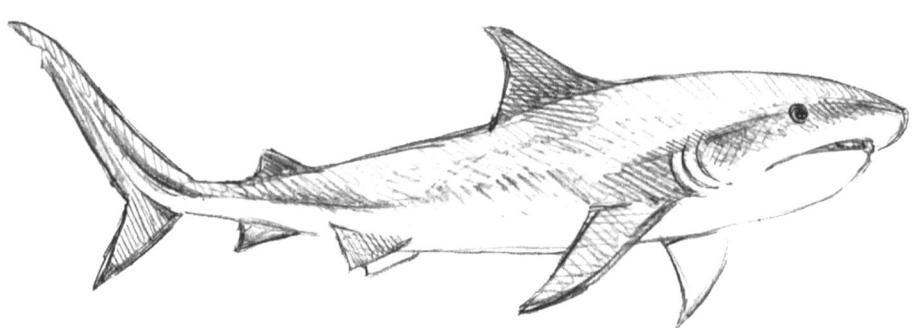

This fish has a nose for navigation because they can detect the magnetic field of the earth. They are better than any other fish or animal at detecting electricity including the electricity that comes from a struggling fish. That is how it finds its food.

Menhaden

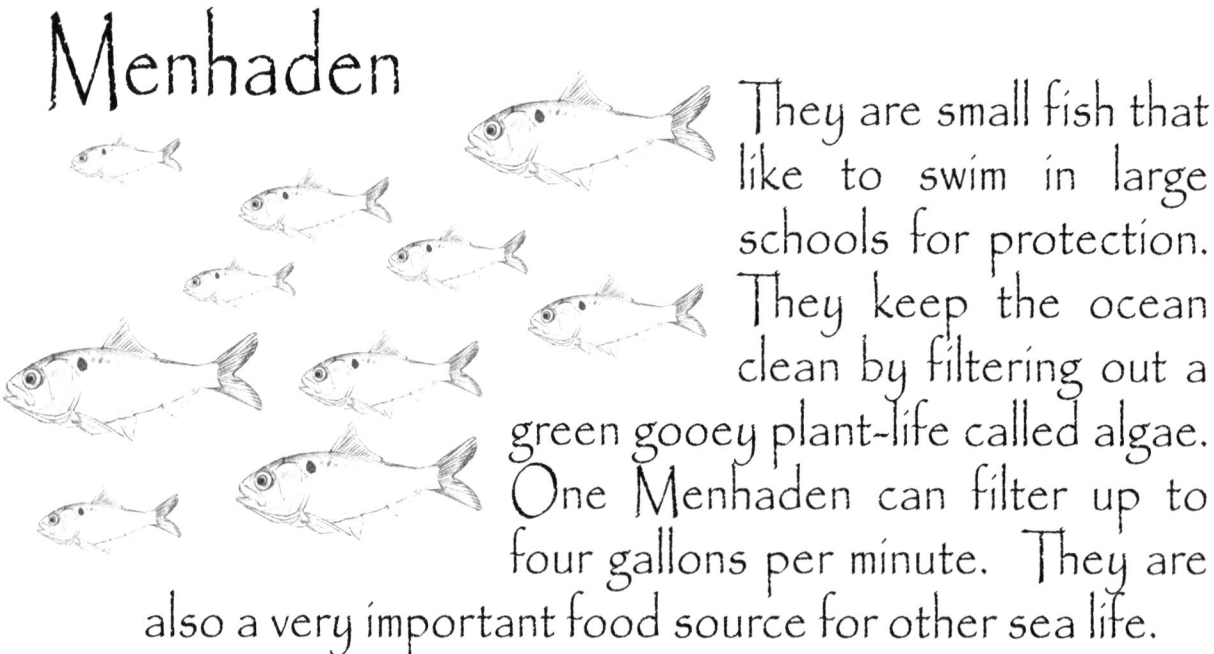

They are small fish that like to swim in large schools for protection. They keep the ocean clean by filtering out a green gooey plant-life called algae. One Menhaden can filter up to four gallons per minute. They are also a very important food source for other sea life.

Paddlefish

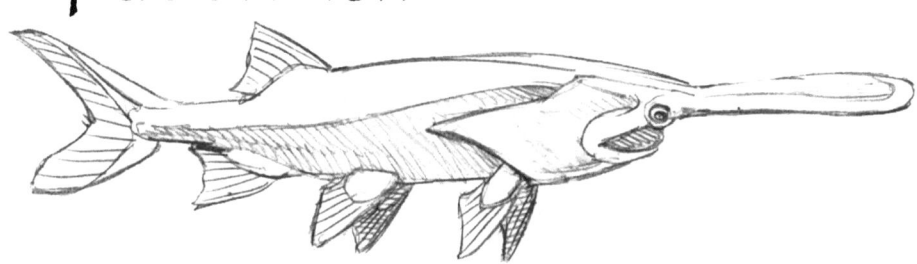

Water glides under that long nose called a "rostrum" and this fish uses it like a bird's wing to prevent it from slipping downward into deeper waters. The Paddlefish eats by swimming with its mouth open and filtering out very small zooplankton, fishes and plant-life.

Striped Marlin

This Fish can move up to 68 miles per hour. That's faster than most speed-limits on highways. It uses its long snout to slash at its prey or to protect itself from predators. Amazingly, it can also change the color of its stripes.

Blue Fin Tuna

Blue Fin Tuna can weigh up to 1,496 pounds (that's about as heavy as a small car)! They can thermoregulate like warm-blooded animals. This means they are able to swim, dine and play in the deep ice-cold water without freezing.

Eels

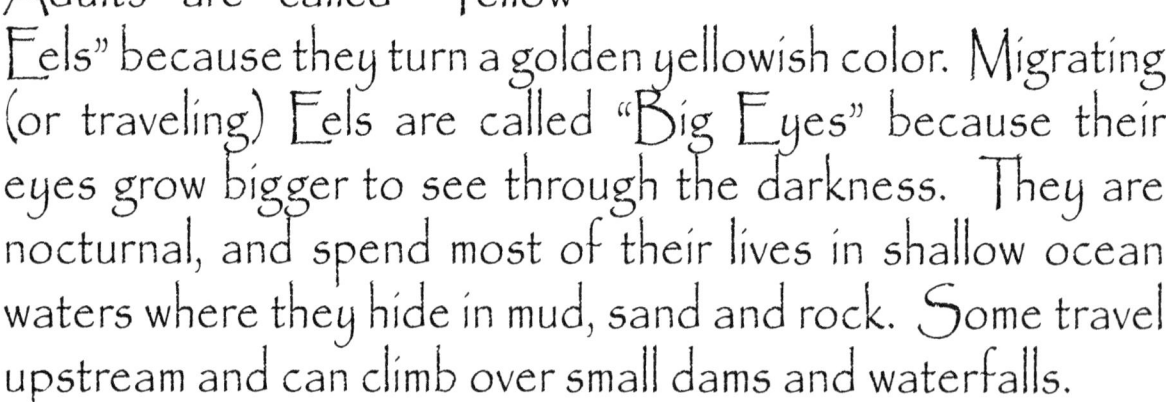

Baby Eels are called "Glass Eels" because they are glassy and see-through. Adults are called "Yellow Eels" because they turn a golden yellowish color. Migrating (or traveling) Eels are called "Big Eyes" because their eyes grow bigger to see through the darkness. They are nocturnal, and spend most of their lives in shallow ocean waters where they hide in mud, sand and rock. Some travel upstream and can climb over small dams and waterfalls.

Skates and Rays

Like Sharks, Skates and Rays also have the ability to sense electricity. This is also how they figure out who each other are (like an electrical fingerprint). Some species like to lay at the bottom of the ocean and hide or stalk prey, others glide about freely near the surface.

Chilean SeaBass

Also known as the Patagonian ToothFish, it lives deep in Arctic water where it's cold and dark. It can do this because its blood acts like antifreeze, and its heart only beats once every six seconds.

Monk Fish

This fish lives in water so dark and so deep, that it has evolved a dangling appendage like a long extra nose with a little light at the tip. It uses this light to attract other fishes and then swallows them whole.

As of this writing, the Monk Fish status was upgraded from "avoid" to "good alternative" by the Monterey Bay Aquarium. This does not mean that the fish is completely out of danger, but it is a step in the right direction.

Notes:

Information found in this book can be located at the sources below. These are also great sources of information if you are interested in learning more about the fishes:

- www.greenpeace.org
- www.iucnredlist.org
- www.montereybayaquarium.org
- www.slowfood.com
- www.sustainablesushi.net
- www.goodfishguide.co.uk
- www.nmfs.noaa.gov/fishwatch/#
- www.blueocean.org
- www.environment.gov.au
- www.amcs.org.au
- animal.discovery.com
- Age determination of orange roughy, Hoplostethus atlanticus (Pisces: Trachichthyidae) using 210Pb:226Ra disequilibria G. E. Fenton, S. A. Short and D. A. Ritz

www.ingramcontent.com/pod-product-compliance
Lightning Source LLC
Chambersburg PA
CBHW041226040426
42444CB00002B/65